THE RIGHT CARE FOR ME

CHEF

KATHLEEN A. KLATTE

ROSEN PUBLISHING

Published in 2025 by The Rosen Publishing Group, Inc.
2544 Clinton Street, Buffalo, NY 14224

Portions of this work were originally authored by Susan Meyer and published as *A Career as a Chef*. All new material in this edition was authored by Kathleen A. Klatte.

Cover Designer: Michael Flynn
Intertior Designer: Rachel Rising
Editor: Kathleen Klatte

Library of Congress Cataloging-in-Publication Data

Names: Klatte, Kathleen A., author.
Title: Chef / Kathleen A. Klatte.
Description: Buffalo : Rosen Publishing, [2025] | Series: The right career for me | Includes index.
Identifiers: LCCN 2023056654 (print) | LCCN 2023056655 (ebook) | ISBN 9781499476286 (library binding) | ISBN 9781499476279 (paperback) | ISBN 9781499476293 (ebook)
Subjects: LCSH: Cooks--Vocational guidance--Juvenile literature. | Cooking--Vocational guidance--Juvenile literature.
Classification: LCC TX652.5 .K579 2025 (print) | LCC TX652.5 (ebook) | DDC 641.5023--dc23/eng/20231213
LC record available at https://lccn.loc.gov/2023056654
LC ebook record available at https://lccn.loc.gov/2023056655

Some of the images in this book illustrate individuals who are models. The depictions do not imply actual situations or events.

Manufactured in the United States of America

CPSIA Compliance Information: Batch #CSRYA25. For further information, contact Rosen Publishing at 1-800-237-9932.

CONTENTS

INTRODUCTION

If there's one thing that everyone everywhere has in common, it's food. We all have to eat, and most people learn to cook because it's a necessary basic skill. But other people look beyond the basics. They wonder what would happen if they added spices to their ground beef before making burgers or how that chef on TV cuts their veggies into such small, precise pieces. They like to visit restaurants and try different foods. Maybe they want to learn how to create gorgeous towering wedding cakes. Or maybe they want to learn how to craft the ultimate comfort food.

Do you like to visit stores that sell different kinds of food? Do you like to ask questions about where different foods come from and how they're made?

If you love food and spending time in the kitchen, a career as a chef might be a good choice for you.

Even in tough economic times, training to be a chef can be a relatively safe choice. Regardless of what else is going on, people have to eat. Of course, it's true that people don't always have to eat the best meals, and they could probably survive on foods they scrounged up and prepared on their own. However, research shows that even in economic downturns people can't help but enjoy themselves by eating at restaurants. Even if they can't afford a fancy sit-down restaurant, people will go to diners, burger joints, and pizzerias. Who doesn't love kicking back and letting someone else cook after a long day? That "someone else" is a trained chef.

You may recall that even at the height of the COVID-19 pandemic, people wanted to go out for meals. Restaurants tried to accommodate this demand safely. They switched to takeout or delivery. They offered simplified menus that could be prepared by fewer cooks. They set up tables on sidewalks or in parking lots—and people came to eat.

According to a recent survey, the average American spends about $166 per month on eating at restaurants. Most of those spend about $11 to $20 per person, per meal. In the last few years, there has been an explosion of chain restaurants that provide convenient, reliable food for the average family. And of course, there's always a percentage of Americans eager to spend upwards of $50 per person, per meal for fine dining.

Unfortunately, many restaurants shut down permanently during the pandemic. Others were able to adapt and design new business plans.

Like many other types of businesses, restaurants are still recovering from the pandemic, and many are operating short-staffed. The Bureau of Labor Statistics (BLS) predicts faster than average growth in the number of jobs available for trained chefs over the next decade.

So, you think you'd like to be a chef—great! But what kind? And where would you like to work? Read on to learn about the sort of education you need to become a chef and what the job is like day-to-day. Don't be afraid to think outside the box. Trained chefs work in many different venues besides restaurants. In fact, almost any place food is served, you'll find a chef.

You'll also learn about the way the culinary and food service industry is changing as more and more people begin to care about what is in their food and where the ingredients they eat come from. First and foremost, the goal is for you to get a definite sense of whether this intense, but rewarding, career path is a good fit for you.

MICHAEL TWITTY AND HISTORIC FOODWAYS

Do you love food? Do you love history too? Did you know it's possible to combine those interests into a career? Some chefs work in living history museums, demonstrating how people cooked in the past and teaching about the sort of foods that were eaten long ago. They talk about the sort of foods that were available, how they were grown, harvested, and stored. Chefs at living history museums generally work in reproduction clothing and use historically appropriate tools and cooking methods.

One of these people is Michael W. Twitty. Twitty won the 2018 James Beard award for his book *The Cooking Gene*. He's a chef and culinary historian who's taught about historic foodways at many living history museums, including Colonial Williamsburg in Williamsburg, Virginia, and Philipsburg Manor in Sleepy Hollow, New York. He also runs a blog called *Afroculinaria* and appeared in the online documentary *People Not Property*.

Twitty traces the roots of American cuisine back to the enslaved people who prepared much of the food in the colonial era. He appears at colonial and antebellum historic sites wearing reproduction clothing and prepares food using tools appropriate to the era of the site. Food might be cooked in copper or cast-iron pots, or on a spit. He might cook on a stove that burns wood or coal, in a fireplace, or even outside over an open fire.

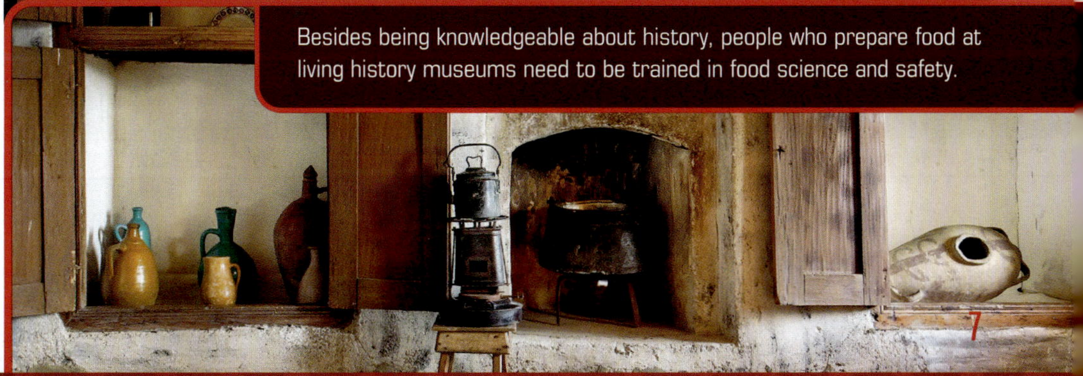

Besides being knowledgeable about history, people who prepare food at living history museums need to be trained in food science and safety.

CHAPTER ONE

SO, YOU WANT TO BE A CHEF

Most people who are interested in a career as a chef started out spending lots of time in their own kitchen. Perhaps a parent showed them how to cook the basics—and how to use the stove and oven safely. Or maybe their grandparents shared cherished family recipes. Or perhaps they were enticed by food magazines on display in the supermarket.

And of course, today, reality cooking shows—as well as their accompanying websites, cookbooks, and other merchandise—are big business. Today's would-be chefs might be encouraged by the images of celebrity chefs with their own TV programs or even unknown home cooks who win competitive shows. The chef's profession is getting much more acclaim and media attention than ever before. You might have seen chefs on television shows who get to meet celebrities and travel the world, all because of their talent in the kitchen. However, it's important to realize that these experiences are not the norm.

Aspiring chefs also need to consider the day-to-day reality of the job. It can be incredibly rewarding for the right person but make no bones about it: it's a lot of hard work. The hours are long, and bosses frequently require you to work nights, weekends, and holidays. While other people are off work and enjoying nice evenings out at restaurants, chefs are the ones helping to make sure they enjoy their leisure time with some delicious food. The job is also physically demanding. As for the working conditions, they are—as you might imagine—hot.

You also need to remember than no one starts at the top. Chefs are responsible for food safety. That includes keeping everything—from dishes and utensils to heavy equipment—clean. Depending on where you work, loading the dishwasher or mopping the floor might be part of your job.

Most chefs discover their love of food and cooking right in their family's kitchen.

WHAT ARE CHEFS MADE OF?

What does it take to become a chef? To begin with you must have a passion for food. Creativity is important, but so is the ability to follow directions. Most people who set their sights on this career do it out of a love for creating new and unique flavor combinations in food. However, you will most likely start in a setting as part of a team producing a menu someone else designed. You must also have a willingness to learn—either in a culinary school or training program or on the job in a kitchen. There are an incredible number of skills that a chef must learn, and the only way to develop these skills and techniques is to practice. A lot of learning to be a chef is simply doing something so many times that it becomes second nature.

Knife skills, for example, are an important part of being a chef. You'll need to learn which knives are used for which tasks, the different styles of cutting vegetables, and how to debone fish and meat. If you've ever seen professional chefs chopping vegetables, you can't help but be impressed by how quickly their hands move and how the pieces they chop are somehow perfectly uniform despite the great knife speed. This skill comes from hours and hours of practice (and more than a few bandages in the early stages). And when they inevitably need those bandages, chefs need to be sure they don't bleed on any food or food preparation surfaces. Chefs need to clean and bandage injuries, and wear gloves.

Chefs need to be aware of what's going on around them at all times. They need to be mindful of food safety no matter how busy the kitchen is.

Raw eggs and meat can carry bacteria that can make people sick, so once a utensil or surface has touched one of these items, it can't be used for anything else until it's been sanitized. Dairy products, fish and meat need to be stored at specific temperatures to be safe for human consumption. Chefs need to be aware of how long perishable ingredients have been sitting out on counters while they work.

Becoming a celebrity chef with your own TV show and merchandise is a fun dream, but it's like winning the lottery—not very likely to happen. Most professional chefs spend most of their working lives cooking in the kitchen, so be sure it's what you're passionate about.

Chefs need to simply enjoy the act of food preparation as its own end rather than a means to an end. It's great to have big dreams, but most chefs spend their time actually working in a kitchen, not in front of a TV camera. If you're hoping to achieve fame and fortune, you probably shouldn't enter the culinary industry. Although there are a ton of reality TV shows chefs can compete on, very few end up with their own show on television or open restaurants in big cities all over the world. For every Emeril Lagasse, Anthony Bourdain, Rachael Ray, or Gordon Ramsay, there are many hundreds of men and women working anonymously all over the country in the kitchens of greasy spoon diners, big name chain eateries, mall food courts, and hotel restaurants. A good chef appreciates food preparation and enjoys providing an essential service to people regardless of where he or she does it.

A good chef must also be creative. This, in part, means that the chef can think outside the box and make new, unique food combinations. Some restaurants serve seasonal menus and others use local ingredients. Chefs in these situations need to work with what's fresh and available. Or in the case of the COVID-19 pandemic, they need to accommodate health department regulations and disrupted supply chains.

A good chef must also be able to work well on a team. Even executive chefs are part of a team—they channel their skills and creativity to bring the owner's vision to life. For example, if they work at a spa or health resort, they need to design menus that are innovative, but healthy. A chef for a head of state is extending their employer's vision of hospitality.

A head chef must be good at delegating responsibilities to the other chefs in the kitchen. The lower chefs must be able to take orders well and carry them out efficiently. Working as a chef is not a good career path for someone who likes to work and succeed alone. The successes or failures of a kitchen on any given night depend upon the whole team.

A chef must work well under pressure. The atmosphere in a kitchen can range from a tense calm to a frenzied excitement. A chef can't be fazed by people yelling orders, tight deadlines, and kitchen mishaps. No matter how careful people try to be, things spill, orders get mixed up, or people send their food back. Every second a chef spends in a kitchen involves a tight deadline. Only a few seconds separate an item that is undercooked from one that is just right or from one that is burned. A good chef is always on his or her toes and displays enormous grace under pressure.

A professional kitchen is orderly and sanitary, no matter how busy it is.

A commercial kitchen is a hot, busy place. Fryers, burners, grills, and even the dishwasher generate lots of heat.

Being a professional chef is a very physical job and training to be a chef can be like boot camp. Chefs are on their feet all night, and not just standing still. They are running back and forth from various burners to counters to the pantry to get more ingredients. There is also the enormous arm strength required to carry out tasks such as chopping 40 pounds (18 kilograms) of potatoes or whisking egg whites into a meringue or deboning 12 ducks. Chefs also need to lift hot, heavy pans from the oven and move cartons of produce. The floor might be slippery from steam, and everything generates heat. Working in a kitchen can be tough, but if you've got what it takes, it can also be a lot of fun.

A HEAD FOR BUSINESS

Being a good cook is one set of skills. Designing full menus is another. And running your own restaurant is a whole different ballgame. If one of your goals in becoming a chef is to own your own restaurant—whether it's a place of your own design or a franchise of a larger chain restaurant—you need to invest time in learning and developing good business skills. However, even if you don't aspire to own a restaurant and are happy operating someone else's kitchen, it's still important to understand how and why a restaurant makes money. It's even more important to understand how and why a restaurant loses money.

Aside from food, restaurant owners are responsible for ordering glassware, cleaning supplies, office supplies, and everything else needed to run the business. What else can you think of?

A restaurant is, first and foremost, a type of business. The only way the business stays open is if it makes enough money to cover all its expenses and pay its staff a competitive wage, ideally with a healthy profit left over. In addition to knowing how to cook, a chef who wants to own a restaurant also must have financial and managerial skills. Just as you can go to school to learn how to cook and prepare food, you can also take classes in learning to run a small business. Business classes are available at community colleges and online.

Most new restaurants fail within a year of opening, and every year many long-established restaurants close. Restaurants can fail for many different reasons. Many of these reasons have nothing to do with the quality of the food. Chef Robert Irvine has a Food Network show called *Restaurant Impossible* where he gives failing restaurants a makeover. One of the most common issues he finds is restaurants that are dirty. The owners haven't factored in scheduling enough time and staff for things to be thoroughly cleaned every day.

Some of the less-than-glamorous details required to run a restaurant include the following:

- a pest control company that conducts inspections at regular intervals
- trash removal
- scheduled professional cleaning of heavy kitchen equipment
- daily, weekly, and monthly cleaning schedules for every part of the restaurant

- professional floor cleaning at regular intervals
- licenses, permits, and insurance

Be honest—how many of those did you think of on your own?

Restaurant owners are also responsible for the outside of the building. This includes hiring companies to wash the windows, maintain the lights and signs, and shovel snow.

While the food is the most important part of any restaurant, it is not the only part. A chef can make the best menu in the world, and the restaurant can still fail if he or she doesn't consider a multitude of other variables. The restaurant must have a good location where it's highly visible and people will be able to get to it easily. It needs safe, convenient parking. It also needs to fit into the neighborhood. Opening a fancy white-linen restaurant in a neighborhood full of low-income housing is pretty much a recipe for disaster. On the other hand, a cool food truck or diner could do very well.

You must assemble and maintain a good staff. Waitstaff, hosts, and other front-of-the-house positions must be filled, as well as all the assistant chef positions in the kitchen. The front-of-the-house positions are just as important as those in the kitchen because these people will interact with customers in a way that the chef and cooks can't. And don't forget bussers and dishwashers!

The restaurant-owning chef also must consider the ambience of the restaurant. The overall feel of the restaurant should be inviting and should complement the food the restaurant serves. You wouldn't want to order a $40 filet mignon in a place with sticky floors and plastic furniture. The look of the restaurant goes a long way to selling the food before it even gets to the plate. And in today's market, you'll also need a website and a full complement of social media sites and someone to manage them.

A restaurant dining room needs to be comfortable for guests, have ample room for staff to serve them, and be easy to clean up after hours.

WHAT DOES A CHEF WEAR?

The iconic image of a chef includes the spotless double breasted white jacket and tall, white hat called a toque. Often, people associate this look with high-end restaurants and hotels. An executive chef might dress this way, especially if they come out of the kitchen to speak to guests.

However, if you watch cooking shows on TV or catch a glimpse behind the scenes of your favorite restaurant, you might notice a more casual look. Jackets might be short-sleeved and tend toward darker colors, such as gray, which hide spills and smudges. Working cooks also tend to wear dark aprons. One thing you'll always see is some kind of hat, often paired with a hair net—this is to comply with health codes concerning loose hair. And of course, comfortable close-toed shoes with good arches and non-slip rubber soles are a must.

Everything a chef wears is designed to help protect them from heat and spills, look neat, and comply with health department regulations.

Everything in an industrial kitchen is designed to be scrubbed and sanitized daily.

LIFE IN THE KITCHEN

Life in a professional kitchen isn't for the faint of heart. Chefs deal with heavy pans and ingredients—from bags of flour to sacks of potatoes—and are on their feet for long periods of time. They're around hot pans, fryers full of hot oil, and scalding steam. In addition to gaining big muscles, new chefs must also learn to grow a thick skin—both literally and figuratively.

They must have a strong and confident personality and learn to take criticism well. In the high-pressure environment of a professional kitchen, even the smallest mistakes are often met with harsh feedback—especially in an upscale restaurant serving expensive cuisine to demanding clients. This isn't true of all kitchens, of course, but for those who don't take constructive criticism well, becoming a chef is not a great career choice. New chefs will make a lot of mistakes before they learn how to do everything right. While they're learning they have to put up with a lot of critical feedback—sometimes being shouted at them at top volume.

Guests paying high prices for fine dining not only expect perfection—they demand it.

A head chef is in charge of a team dedicated to providing all of their guests with a wonderful dining experience.

THE BUCK STOPS HERE

A chef's day is very long—especially for a head chef and even more for one who has an ownership stake in the business. A chef at an average-sized restaurant might arrive at nine or ten o'clock in the morning to make sure the necessary produce, meats, and other foods were delivered overnight. In restaurants that host banquets or private parties, they need to keep track of what's needed for those as well. If there are problems, the chef might have to call the restaurant's suppliers to complain. If any kitchen staff have called out, they need to redistribute tasks or call someone in. They might need to consult with the owner or have a team meeting to start the day.

Mid-morning, the chef might start preparing (or supervising the preparation of) sauces and desserts or any food items that require a long time to cook. Around 11:30 a.m., the restaurant will open for lunch and the chef will need to start cranking out dishes for the busy lunch rush, which usually lasts until 2 p.m. After lunch, many things need to be cleaned and reset for dinner. From 2 p.m. until 4 p.m., the head chef might have time to review stocks and see what the kitchen needs to order. At 4 p.m., he or she can go over the specials for the evening with the sous-chefs and the waitstaff.

Depending on the restaurant, the dinner rush can last anywhere from 6 p.m. to 10 p.m. or 11 p.m. After the last meal is served and the last customer is seen happily out the door, the chef can supervise cleanup and prep for the next day. Only then can he or she head home around midnight or later to get a few hours of sleep and begin the whole process again the next day.

A professional kitchen during dinner service demands full concentration from all team members!

AN INTERVIEW WITH CHEF DIANE REEDER (CULINARY INSTITUTE OF AMERICA CLASS OF 2019 AND OWNER OF THE KINGSTON CANDY BAR)

You were already an established professional when you completed your training at CIA. How has having the "magic piece of paper" impacted your career?
"Having an associate of culinary science from the CIA definitely upped my credibility in the culinary industry."

You've done a lot of work to help the hungry with compassion and dignity. Can you tell me about some of the projects you've worked on?
"During the Clinton administration, I canvassed for support of the Bill Emerson Good Samaritan Food Donation Act. This is a law that offers limited liability protection to retailers and restaurants that donate unused food for distribution to needy individuals.

"I was also invited to the White House to meet former first lady Michelle Obama as part of her Chefs Move to Schools initiative for healthy school lunches.

"I ran a soup kitchen called the Queen's Galley in Kingston, New York, for several years. It was a groundbreaking program that served three meals a day, 365 days a year. Meals were served in courses, like a restaurant, on real plates. Clients didn't need to prove their need—just sit and eat and be treated with dignity and respect. This model is gaining a foothold among other aid societies."

A few years ago, you helped grant a wish for a Make-a-Wish child. What was your favorite part of that project?

"That was a 12-course royal feast served in a castle. My husband Jay provided costumes for the young queen and her princess, as well as the servers. We pulled out all the stops to make it as memorable as possible. The desert course included edible sugar balloons that were floated out to the dining room, and ice cream made at table side with liquid nitrogen.

"Of course, in the middle of the meal there was a poignant reminder of why we were doing this when an alarm went off and the child's mother had to administer her medication."

Tell me about your current endeavor, the Kingston Candy Bar.

"The Kingston Candy Bar is a retirement project. When I ran the Queen's Galley, clients often had serious, complex problems they needed help with. It's draining to deal with that on a daily basis. At the Candy Bar, people come in just looking for some sweet thing to make them happy. I'm delighted to help with that."

Being a chef is all about details—from choosing the freshest sources of ingredients to garnishing the plate.

CHAPTER TWO

A WEALTH OF OPTIONS

As mentioned before, very few chefs will have the right combination of skills, personality, and just plain luck to have a celebrity career. And not everyone wants to deal with all the fuss and details of running their own business. So what else is there? There is a wealth of different options available in the culinary industry. Learning more about these career choices can help you focus on which opportunities best suit your individual goals and interests.

Your main goal in choosing to be a chef should simply be that you enjoy making good food. Next you need to consider things such as how much time you want to devote to your career—do you want to be the person who gets called at weird hours because something needs fixing right now? Or do you want to focus on cooking? Do you want to experiment with new flavors and ingredients or perfect old favorites? There are no wrong answers. We will look at all the different kinds of chefs and all the places you might find them—from restaurants, cruise ships, and hotels to private homes and even grocery stores.

DIFFERENT KINDS OF KITCHENS

Not all chefs wear pristine white jackets and toques and issue orders in French. Often, they wear aprons with their company's logo. They might wear a hairnet or a little paper hat. They may work in a chain restaurant, that fancy hotel where people book events, or for that cool new food truck. Wherever people gather to eat, you'll find a chef dedicated to serving them good food.

Most people picture chefs in upscale settings such as white-linen restaurants, overseeing classic cuisine or developing sophisticated new dishes. But that's only one setting where chefs work.

These chefs are grilling sausages at a street food festival.

You can also find them at hotels, resorts, and cruise ships. Resorts and cruise ships often contain multiple restaurants as well as large dining rooms. A hotel offers a great variety of opportunities for a chef. Hotel kitchens are often very structured and large because they serve hundreds if not thousands of guests. When working in a hotel kitchen, a chef is not just preparing breakfast, lunch, and dinner, but also buffets, brunches, and room service, and catering for weddings, conferences, and other special events.

Another place you'll find chefs is catering halls. These are large facilities that host events such as weddings. They often have a large ballroom that can be arranged with tables, a dance floor, and a stage for a band or DJ. Other chefs specialize in off-site catering—that is, they go to a client's site, perhaps even a private house, to cook for an event. They might not know what the kitchen they'll be working in will be like until they get there. They must travel with all of their tools. And most difficult of all, they must serve a huge number of people all at once.

The food served in school cafeterias has improved greatly in recent years, as new emphasis has been placed on healthy options and fresh, quality ingredients. During her tenure, former first lady Michelle Obama crusaded for healthier school lunches. Cafeteria cooks work not only in schools, but also in colleges, office buildings, nursing homes, and hospitals all over the country. They have the difficult job of making mass amounts of food for a huge group of people. And this food should be characterized not just by its quantity, but also by its quality.

Cafeteria chefs, especially in medical facilities, may also have to follow stricter health and nutrition guidelines that will alter how their food will taste. Ingredients such as sodium and sugar can affect patients with conditions including diabetes and high blood pressure. In a nursing home setting, there may be patients with dentures or other dental issues who have difficulty chewing. Older people can also be fussy about trying new foods. And of course, the healthiest food in the world won't help a patient unless they eat it—it needs to look and smell good, even to an ill or confused person.

Since the COVID-19 pandemic, many stores have replaced salad bars and buffets with grab-and-go cases. Cooks prepare and package the food for sale in the store instead of customers serving themselves from open containers.

Chefs in cafeterias often have to follow specific nutritional guidelines, while still making sure their food is appealing.

Another place it's easy for chefs to go unnoticed is in grocery stores. While most people who are grocery shopping focus on all the food that they have to go home and cook themselves, think about some of the food in the store that's already made. Even the smallest local grocery store has a grab-and-go section these days. Although many stores eliminated salad bars and other serve-yourself options due to the pandemic, most stores have prepackaged salads, sandwiches, and even entrées. All that food had to be prepared, cooked, and packaged by a chef. If the deli counter has prepared pasta salads or preseasoned meats, a chef had to make those, too. And what grocery store would be complete without a bakery? A chef made those breads and desserts that are so hard to resist.

At the other end of the spectrum are chefs who cook for just one family. Personal chefs usually work in their employers' homes. They are completely in charge of the preparation of meals, usually even choosing and buying the ingredients. They must plan a menu based on the preferences, schedule, dietary restrictions, and allergies of the family for whom they cook. This type of job can allow a personal chef greater freedom and more time off than that enjoyed by his or her restaurant colleagues.

DIFFERENT KINDS OF CHEFS

You may notice that many French words are used in the culinary industry This is because a lot of these terms and titles originated in France with Auguste Escoffier, but today they are used in kitchens all over the world. The word chef comes from the French phrase *chef de cuisine* which means "chief of the kitchen" in English. Today, the word chef has come to mean not just the head of the kitchen, but any culinary professional regardless of his or her rank. The titles executive chef or head chef are used to identify the person who is truly the kitchen chief.

The tall white hat chef's wear is called a toque, which is a French word derived from Arabic. In more formal kitchens, the height of the chef's hat denotes their rank. The executive chef is the ultimate authority in the kitchen; therefore, they wear the tallest hat. They decide what should be on the menu and how it should be prepared, right down to how it should appear on the plate. They manage the kitchen staff and are also often in charge of the ordering and purchasing of inventory—deciding what foods to buy and whom to buy them from. An executive chef may manage more than one restaurant, particularly in a venue such as a resort. A chef de cuisine is in charge of the kitchen of a single restaurant.

Working under the executive chef is the sous-chef. In fact, sous-chef literally means "under chief" in French. The sous-chef is the second-in-command in the kitchen. This person is responsible for carrying out the executive chef's orders and instructions. The sous-chef is also familiar with every position in the kitchen and can step into any of them. Sometimes the head chef is the owner of the restaurant. In these cases, the sous-chef might actually be in charge of running the kitchen, while the head chef is occupied with running the restaurant as a whole. Smaller restaurants may not have a sous-chef, but large restaurants may have more than one—a day sous-chef and a night sous-chef. The sous-chef, as the second most important person in the kitchen, usually gets to handle the most expensive ingredients that some of the lower chefs don't get to work with.

An executive chef is responsible for everything that comes out of their kitchen, down to the smallest piece of garnish.

CLUB DES CHEFS DES CHEFS

The Club des Chefs des Chefs (CCC) is considered the most exclusive culinary organization in the world. Its membership consists of the personal chefs of heads of state, or the executive chef of the venue that hosts state events, such as the White House or Buckingham Palace. Current membership includes Mark Flanagan, head chef of the Royal Household (Great Britain) and Cristeta Comerford, White House executive chef.

Gilles Bragard founded the organization in 1977 to support the role that food and chefs play in international diplomacy. It's headquartered in Paris, France.

A sous-chef works their way up to the position by learning every aspect of the kitchen and menu. Their duties may include ordering supplies, training new staff, and expediting during lunch or dinner service. In the chef world, expediting means helping to pace the meals so that they go out of the kitchen at the right time. It's often a difficult juggling act to make sure the food for each table goes out at the same time and at the optimum temperature. They examine each dish before it leaves the kitchen.

Below the sous-chef are the *chefs de parties*, also known as the line cooks or station cooks. Each line cook is in charge of a certain station in the kitchen. Say you go to a nice restaurant and order a steak that comes with a side of green beans. You also order a shrimp cocktail to start. If it is a large restaurant, your meal may be made by several different cooks. One line cook might man the grill to make sure your steak comes out perfectly, while another might be in charge of cooking vegetables, and yet another prepares the shellfish. Everyone in a kitchen has to work as a team to make sure every customer's order is prepared correctly and sent out at just the right temperature and the right time. The person who calls for the necessary dishes and prepares the trays for the wait staff is called the *aboyeur* or expediter.

There are even more kinds of chefs under the umbrella of station cooks because the chef who works at each station has a different title. The person who cooked your steak? That's the grill chef. The creator of your green beans was likely the sauté chef (sometimes known by the French word *saucier*) who is in charge of all sautéed items and their sauces. A tournant is a chef who can step in anywhere and help at any station.

A professional chef knows how to prepare great food with flair.

A fresh and appetizing salad sets the tone for the rest of the dining experience.

The culinary professional who plates salads is known as the garde-manger. The garde-manger is in charge of preparing cold items from salads to cold appetizers. The garde-manger is often considered a starting position in the kitchen because there is less training required to prepare some of these foods. Nevertheless, the garde-manger is a vitally important part of the kitchen staff. After all, the foods from the garde-manger's station are often responsible for the diners' first impressions of the meal.

After the appetizer and entrée, there's one more type of chef who handles the meal's final impression. If you still have any room left after your steak and you choose to order a dessert, it would be prepared by the pastry chef.

JUST DESSERTS

In some settings, the *pâtissier* or pastry chef might be responsible for baking the restaurant's bread, but generally the title is reserved for the chef who creates desserts. Unlike bakers, who follow recipes devised by others, pastry chefs create their own recipes. Of course, they bake things such as cakes and sweet pastries, but they also craft other sweet treats including ice cream and sorbet.

Unlike other cooks, a pastry chef is somewhat independent. In some settings, they're supervised by the executive chef. In others, they may have their own staff. Regardless, the pastry chef's creations have to fit into the overall theme of the restaurant.

Aside from creating the recipes for their desserts, pastry chefs also design the presentation. This might include swirls of sauce or sugar-dusted berries on the plate.

A pastry chef's creations are a feast for all the senses.

It takes a great deal of practice to master professional knife techniques.

Below the station cook is the commis. The commis is an assistant or apprentice to the station cook. This is an entry-level position. The commis can learn valuable skills from the cook under whom they're working. They can gain valuable knife and food preparation skills while experiencing the fast pace and pressures of a real kitchen environment. In a large kitchen, a commis chef will eventually work at and master each station.

Similar to the commis, but not always thought of as an apprentice position, is the prep cook. In many ways the prep cook is the backbone of the kitchen. He or she does a lot of the more basic, humble, physically grueling but essential tasks, such as chopping all the vegetables for the night or mincing all the garlic. They might be involved in moving heavy supplies or cleaning. The prep cook might even butcher some of the less expensive cuts of meat so they'll be ready when the more experienced chefs are ready to use them.

As you can see, there are many paths available to a trained chef. Take some time to think about what you'd like to do. Serving crowds in a cafeteria setting requires creativity to create appealing food that meets the necessary nutritional guidelines. Catering weddings and other events can be a very high-pressure environment requiring tact and diplomacy, as well as culinary skills. Is there a particular type of cuisine you're passionate about? Or maybe you're interested in a cozy diner or coffee shop. Again, there are no wrong answers

Professional chefs take great pride in presenting beautifully plated delicious meals.

CRISTETA COMERFORD WHITE HOUSE EXECUTIVE CHEF

Cristeta Comerford has been the White House executive chef since 2005. She's the first woman, first Asian American, and first person of color to hold the position.

Comerford was born in Manila in 1962 and studied food technology at the University of the Philippines. She began working as an assistant chef at the White House in 1995 for Executive Chef Walter Scheib during the Clinton administration. Former first lady Laura Bush appointed her executive chef in 2005. Since then, she's held the position under the Obama, Trump, and Biden administrations. She's a member of the Club des Chefs des Chefs. Her salary is about $100,000 per year.

The White House executive chef is responsible for feeding the first family and their guests. Sometimes those guests include visiting heads of state.

CHAPTER THREE

BEYOND RECIPES

Once you've decided to become a chef, the next step is to decide where you'd like to train. There are other options besides a formal culinary school. Many successful chefs have risen to the top of their profession by starting at the bottom, as line and prep cooks and even dishwashers. They worked their way up without any formal education in culinary arts. Many of the skills you need to become a whiz with a knife or whip up perfect sauces can be learned right in the kitchen at whatever restaurant hires you.

You need to think about what kind of career you'd like to have and what resources you have to pay for your training. Community colleges and trade schools offer classes in professional cooking and baking. Generally, these are shorter than a degree program and culminate in a certificate. Depending on where you live or what kind of facility you want to work in, you may need to take a food safety certification such as ServSafe. Of course, a first aid certification is always a useful thing to have. There are also four-year college programs to consider.

If you have your sights set on a career as an executive chef or your interests lie in high-end cuisine, culinary school is probably a good choice. The formal training you will receive, sometimes from highly regarded industry professionals, can be invaluable, as can the opportunity to be exposed to a wide range of kitchen settings, cooking styles and techniques, and culinary traditions and tastes. Of course, there are some drawbacks to a culinary arts education, such as cost. If you decide this is the right path for you, you need to consider the various schools and what their requirements are.

Formal culinary arts programs include classes in business as well as food safety and food science.

CULINARY SCHOOL

Doctors go to medical school and lawyers go to law school. Once they reach a certain stage of their training, they move on to working in hospitals and law offices. But what about chefs? If you choose to attend culinary school, you will learn some of the history and methods behind culinary arts, but most of what you will be doing is hands-on experiential learning. In fact, at the Culinary Institute of America (CIA) students run restaurants that are open to the paying public.

At a culinary school you can learn new skills in a controlled environment. You can also learn both local and global techniques. If you are working at a restaurant in a small Midwestern town hundreds of miles from the nearest big city, you might not have the same access to the increasingly popular and in-demand techniques of Malaysian cuisine, for example, or South American taste traditions. Formal academic training will give you a much broader range of knowledge, skills, techniques, and culinary references. You will also have hands-on, supportive, personalized help and be working with teachers whose primary goal is to mold you into a better chef. Formal programs often include at least an introduction to the business aspect of running a restaurant.

Another advantage of formal training is that it is often part of a college or university program that allows students to work toward official certification as a chef. Upon graduation, when you are looking for your first job, you will already be recognized as a chef. This might help you start a few rungs up the ladder. Not only will you possibly be able to start in a higher position in the kitchen, but you might also be eligible for a higher starting salary. For example, according to the Bureau of Labor Statistics (BLS) a cook (who might not have a degree) might earn about $31,000 per year. A head cook or chef (who would be expected to have a degree) might earn around $57,000 per year. Additionally, going to culinary school can help you make valuable connections in the restaurant world. You will get a well-rounded sense of culinary history and learn several different techniques and traditions.

Students at a culinary school learn all the latest techniques and train on professional-grade equipment.

Choosing to attend culinary school is a big decision. Much like medical school or law school, the cost must be considered. For example, tuition at the CIA can run in excess of $20,000 per semester. Although there are shorter (and less prestigious) culinary training programs you can join, most degree-granting programs require two to four years of study to earn certification. Additionally, the cost of culinary school is much higher than other methods of training. Of course, student loans and scholarships are always an option. Unlike receiving your culinary training on the job, you are not getting paid when you attend culinary school. In fact, you are paying—often quite handsomely—to enroll in the classes. You might also be required to complete an externship. This is similar to an internship in that you shadow a professional chef. Externships are generally unpaid. When you graduate from culinary school, you will still have to pay your dues in the kitchen. While culinary school might give you the knowledge, techniques, experience, and certification to start a little higher in the kitchen hierarchy and

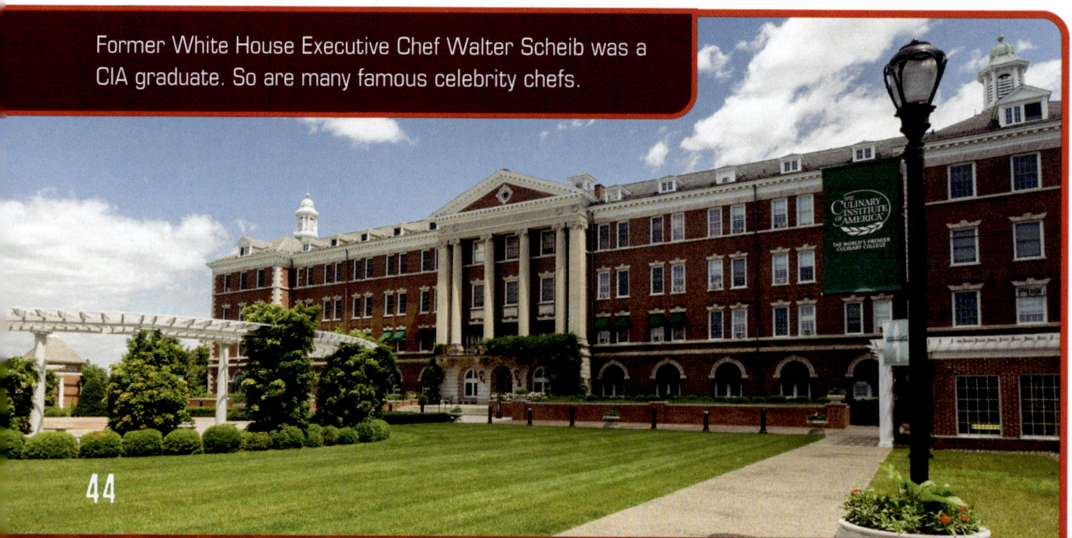

Former White House Executive Chef Walter Scheib was a CIA graduate. So are many famous celebrity chefs.

rise a little faster, it still takes a lot of hard work, long hours, and low wages to become a high-ranking chef.

Admission to the top culinary schools is very competitive. You need to consider the application requirements and cost and compare then to the type of career you'd like to have. Make sure to do your research and learn what sort of credentials the school will offer you and if it is well known and respected in the culinary world. Try to find information on how many of the program's graduates get placed in culinary jobs soon after graduation and if the school boasts any alumni who have become prominent professionals in the field. For example, the CIA's graduates include many famous TV chefs and a former White House executive chef.

WHERE DO YOU WANT TO STUDY?

Once you decide to pursue a degree or diploma from a culinary program, you still have options to consider. There are several questions you must ask yourself to help choose a program that will be a good fit. Are you interested in attending—and can you afford—a two- or a four-year program? What is your budget for attending a culinary program? Do you want to go full-time or part-time? During the day or in the evening? Do you want to live on campus or commute from home? (Bear in mind that going away to school can double the costs.) What type of cooking are you interested in focusing on or specializing in? For example, the Escoffier School of Culinary Arts (ICE) offers a diploma in plant-based cuisine at their Boulder, Colorado, campus and CIA offers a major in wine and beverage management.

A sommelier is a wine expert. Most culinary schools will have at least an introduction to wines. Some offer it as a major.

There are a great number of culinary schools out there with good reputations that you can attend. There is an option to suit any aspiring chef's schedule, budget, and needs. There are four-year degree programs that offer bachelor's degrees and other nondegree courses that offer certificates that might take only a few months. Escoffier offers a variety of courses online. And don't forget to check out state university options—you can get a solid culinary education without breaking the bank. The downside of this great variety of options is that it can be hard to pick the perfect one.

One of the most well-known culinary programs in the United States is the Culinary Institute of America. This four-year university is the oldest culinary school in the United States. It was founded in 1946 in Connecticut. Today, however, it is located in Hyde Park, New York. It also has campuses in California, Texas, and Singapore. Over the years, the school has produced over 35,000 new chefs, including former White House Executive Chef Walter Scheib (1954–2015). The CIA is a residential school, meaning students live on campus while learning all about the world of culinary arts.

The CIA is a well-respected program both in the United States and around the world. It offers a well-rounded program that covers everything from American and international cooking techniques to nutrition science and sanitation, as well as hospitality and restaurant management. The goal of the institution is to produce well-rounded chefs ready for their first job in any kitchen. The program also requires students to work in one of four on-campus restaurants and complete a one-semester externship. An externship is like an internship, but usually shorter in duration and often set up by an institution. It is a period of time spent working in a restaurant for the purpose of gaining practical experience. An externship, like an internship, can be paid or unpaid. Students also have the option to study abroad.

While the CIA is the oldest culinary school in the country, it is far from the only top-notch institution. Johnson & Wales University in Providence, Rhode Island (with other locations in Charleston, South Carolina, and Norfolk, Virginia), is a well-regarded school that offers associate's, bachelor's, and graduate degrees in food service and hospitality.

Auguste Escoffier (1846–1935) was an innovative chef who modernized French cuisine. Today the Escoffier School of Culinary Arts has campuses in Boulder, Colorado, and Austin, Texas.

Another leading culinary arts program is the Institute of Culinary Education in New York City, which offers 8- to 13-month career training programs in culinary arts, pastry and baking arts, plant-based culinary arts, restaurant and culinary management, and hospitality and hotel management. It was founded by Peter Kump, a founding member of the James Beard Foundation, an organization devoted to culinary excellence. There is an additional campus in Los Angeles, California, as well as online programs.

COOKING FOR THE TROOPS

Another way to become trained as a chef is through the armed forces. Soldiers, sailors, and airmen all need to eat, so there's always a need for trained cooks. But get that fellow from *M.A.S.H.* slopping unidentifiable stuff onto metal trays out of your mind! Today's military focuses on good nutrition for the troops, so military chefs are trained to prepare restaurant-quality meals.

In fact, military chefs have competed on—and won—the Food Network show *Chopped*. And the U.S Navy operates the mess inside the White House. Like other military career paths, culinary specialist training prepares personnel for rewarding civilian careers after they leave the service. In addition, they don't incur student debt. This training is available for enlisted personnel as well as members of the National Guard. Like other military career paths, there are required minimum scores for certain parts of the Armed Services Vocational Aptitude Battery (ASVAB) and candidates must complete basic training.

Chef Andre Rush is a U.S. Army veteran and celebrity chef. He's won many awards and worked as a chef in the White House.

GETTING IN

Top culinary schools are very competitive. It's important to check out their requirements early to make sure you're taking the classes you need. If your high school offers any sort of cooking or culinary classes, that's probably a good start. Cooks measure things all the time, and they need to be able to extrapolate quantities of ingredients, so make sure you're taking appropriate math and science classes, especially chemistry.

The CIA requires high school transcripts, letters of recommendation, an essay explaining why the applicant wishes to study culinary arts, and a résumé with the applicant's background in the food service industry. Not all culinary schools ask for a background in the food service industry as a prerequisite for application. The CIA, however, requires a minimum of three to five months of food service experience, at least some of which must have been in a professional kitchen.

Make sure to do your research when looking for the culinary school that is the perfect fit for you. Visit their websites and read any brochures and literature they have available. Look at their courses and see if they cover a range of techniques and skills, particularly those you're most interested in learning. Be sure to ask your guidance counselor for help. It's literally their job to help you research schools and financial options. It's also important to consider the cost of the program and if it's within your reach. Will you be able to work part- or full-time while studying, or will the program require all your time and attention? The answer to this question will determine how you budget for tuition costs and living expenses. If your finances dictate that you need to work, investigate online options. Many schools added or expanded online courses during the pandemic.

Finally, consider what you will be taking away from any program. Will you have a meaningful and valuable certificate from a recognized and reputable culinary institution? Does the program offer professional connections and employment assistance or job placement after graduation? Will it give you the opportunity to intern or work in restaurants while in school? Don't be afraid to ask a lot of questions when you go to visit schools. If you can't visit all the schools you're interested in, make sure to contact an admissions officer or academic adviser with any questions you have. You can also watch videos on YouTube. The CIA and Escoffier schools have official accounts with lots of interesting content.

At culinary school you'll not only learn skills, you'll make great professional connections.

AN INTERVIEW WITH CHEF OLIVIA REEDER (CULINARY INSTITUTE OF AMERICA CLASS OF 2023 BACHELOR OF CULINARY SCIENCE)

When did you know you wanted to be a chef?
"Not until recently. I was curious because of my mom, who'd graduated with an associate of culinary science in 2019. I'm also competitive and wanted to complete the bachelor's degree."

Did you look at other culinary schools before applying to CIA?
"No. Just CIA. I was familiar with the campus from visiting with my mom and I'd even met some of the faculty."

What's your favorite thing about culinary school?
"I really like to feed people. I don't cook much for myself, but I love to cook for other people."

What's most challenging?
"The schedule can be very hectic. Sometimes you don't get the schedule you want or need. Sometimes one class or prerequisite can really mess up your schedule."

What do you plan to do after graduation?
"I'm not sure right now. I've worked as an apprentice at Sushi Makio for a few years. It's been a great experience and opened many doors for me, including an invitation to travel to Japan and work there."

Plant-based cuisine is one of the majors offered in major culinary schools today.

CHAPTER FOUR

LANDING YOUR FIRST JOB

Completing a culinary program is a tremendous achievement. However, there's a big difference between the controlled environment of a school and the real world. No matter how fine the establishment where you go to work is, it's still subject to things such as missing or wrong deliveries, equipment breaking down, and power outages or water main breaks. And then there's people. Sometimes staff members call out at the last minute or don't pull their weight. Customers will find things to complain about, no matter how good the food or service is. It takes time and experience to learn how to deal with all these factors.

This is why every chef starts at (or near) the bottom and works their way up through patience, perseverance, and practice. Ever wondered what Emeril Lagasse's first job in the food industry was? Emeril—who is now the author of several books, owns multiple restaurants, and has a long-running cooking show—started washing pots and pans in a bakery. Dieter Schorner, who was named one of the top pastry chefs in the world by *Time* magazine, started out salting pretzels. And Judy Rodgers, who has published cookbooks from her acclaimed San

Francisco restaurant, the Zuni Cafe, started out working in a Dairy Queen.

Regardless of what school you graduate from or what type of degree you earn, you won't start off running your own restaurant or hotel. You still need to work your way up through the ranks. First jobs are an important learning experience. One of the first things that every chef must learn is to be humble and to bring the same enthusiasm and attention to detail to any task, no matter how small or basic. From making sure each pretzel is expertly salted to mopping the floors of a fast-food restaurant, every job is important. Each job should be treated as a learning experience that creates customer satisfaction—and a better chef.

Waitstaff take the brunt of complaints, but in a high-end restaurant, a chef may need to speak to a customer. It takes experience to learn how to handle this type of situation with tact and diplomacy.

Textbooks and classroom study can't prepare you for everything you'll encounter in the workplace. Textbook customer service leans toward "the customer is always right." Reality dictates that sometimes guests have too much to drink, behave disruptively, or complain in hopes of getting a free meal. It takes time and experience to develop the judgment to assess each situation properly. There are tools that can help, such as state-mandated training for alcohol servers. (You may be required to take this training even if your job is centered in the kitchen.)

INTERNSHIPS, EXTERNSHIPS, AND APPRENTICESHIPS

Once you've chosen a career, naturally you want to start being paid as soon as possible. Some people choose to immediately check out a job posting website and look for paying work. Others may choose to complete an internship, externship, or apprenticeship. There are no wrong choices. It's all about deciding what's more likely to get you the kind of career you want.

An internship is a short-term professional placement—usually for a summer or a semester. Interns get real-world experience and professional recommendations. An externship is a similar experience—externs shadow a professional to learn more about their chosen industry. Internships and externships may or may not be paid positions, but they can definitely be included on your resume.

Another option is an apprenticeship. Apprentices don't just observe—they're mentored by a master in the industry. Some of these opportunities offer credentials just like culinary school programs. This means that, even for those chefs who opted to forgo culinary school, they will have official certification of the acquisition of required skills and experience they can put on their résumés when they look for jobs. The reasons for choosing to apprentice rather than attend culinary school can vary.

For example, Job Corps is a program that offers free apprenticeships in a variety of industries including food service and hospitality. Training is free for qualified applicants—generally at-risk teens. The investment of time and money might keep some chefs out of the classroom, while others might find learning through hands-on, real-world professional experience to be a better fit for them. Apprenticeships are also available through the National Restaurant Association and American Culinary Federation (ACF).

You can learn plenty from an entry-level job. However, an apprenticeship is specifically designed to be a learning opportunity.

Even if you can't afford an expensive culinary education there are training programs available. Hard work goes a long way!

The concept of apprenticeship dates back at least as far as medieval Europe. Traditionally, French chefs, some as young as 13 years old, would learn the ways of cooking from master chefs. This system has remained largely unchanged in Europe, but the American apprenticeship system is less developed. There are fewer restaurants in the United States that are willing to take on novice chefs and train them, and laws in this country restrict the age of apprentices and limit how much they can work without pay. However, an exception is the ACF, which runs a three-year national apprenticeship training program for culinary students in the United States. The National Restaurant Association's program is run in partnership with the Department of Labor (DOL).

For those who don't want or are unable to land a coveted apprenticeship, the best way to really kick-start a culinary career is to land your first job. There's no substitute for the kind of hands-on education and experience you can get in a kitchen. As you begin to look for a job, there are many things to consider. Where would you like to work? And what sort of opportunities are available where you live? Small town restaurants often have trouble finding good help, so there may be less competition for these positions. In a small restaurant, you'll be exposed to all aspects of the business. However, the greatest concentration of restaurants, and particularly critically acclaimed restaurants, is usually in urban areas where the cost of living is much higher. If you do land a job at a top restaurant, don't expect a top-dollar salary to go with it. Because training under renowned chefs is considered a valuable learning experience, and because competition for these positions is so high, there's a good chance that the pay level is inversely proportional to the status of the restaurant.

A good mentor is an invaluable asset to a beginning chef.

JAMES BEARD

James Beard (1903–1985) was an American chef and cookbook author. His preferred cuisine consisted of simple American and English fare. He was one of the first chefs to appear on television. Throughout his career, he wrote more than 20 cookbooks, many of which are still in print today. In 1955, he opened his own cooking school in New York.

Today, the James Beard Foundation awards scholarships to aspiring chefs. The foundation also presents the annual James Beard awards for excellence in the restaurant industry.

The James Beard Foundation Awards are presented to outstanding chefs, restaurants, and cookbooks.

Maybe you have an idea of what sort of restaurant you'd like to work in. A bigger restaurant will have a larger staff and turn out a high number of dishes each night. But without previous training or experience, you might be starting out as a dishwasher or busser. However, a smaller restaurant, one with fewer chefs in the kitchen, may give you the opportunity of taking on greater and more varied responsibilities because there are so few "hands on deck." Working at a hotel can also provide a wide variety of restaurant and kitchen experiences. No matter where your first job is, however, you will learn a lot. Sometimes you learn what kind of setting you don't want to work in—and that's also valuable knowledge.

Given so many options, it can be difficult to choose where you want to work. A good rule of thumb is to simply look for jobs at the places that interest you most. If you want to be a pastry chef, you should look for jobs in pastry shops or restaurants where you could work under a strong pastry chef. If you want to work in a restaurant, you should look for the type of restaurant where you feel most comfortable and whose menu and cooking styles you most admire. Do you eat there? Would you bring your family there? Set your sights on a kitchen where you can get the best possible learning experience. Much like picking a culinary school, choosing a place to learn or continue learning will benefit your overall culinary education, even if it is not the highest-paying position.

And of course, you might not be interested in a restaurant at all. Another venue might be better suited to the kind of career you want. This might include:

- **Schools**. Elementary and high schools have cafeterias. College campuses often have multiple dining options.
- **Hospitals.** Hospitals provide food for patients. Larger hospitals might also have a food court for visitors and a cafeteria for staff.
- **Nursing homes or other residential facilities.** Depending on the facility, food might be served to residents on trays, or there might be a dining room or even a restaurant. Possibly a combination of options.
- **Catering companies.** If you're interested in events, rather than day-to-day meals, a catering hall might be a good choice.
- **Amusement facilities or historic sites.** Pretty much any place people congregate has some sort of food service. Why not combine interests?

Yes—even the people who make funnel cakes are trained professionals!

RÉSUMÉS AND INTERVIEWS

The first step in any job hunt is to create your résumé. It's important to emphasize all academic, volunteer, internship, and work experience that could be applicable and demonstrate your love of and passion for food. This is especially true if you are a new chef who might not have a long list of direct restaurant experience to put down. If you're attending a trade or culinary school, there might be someone who helps with job placement. If so, you should take advantage. Libraries and other community education programs often have résumé writing classes. There are also templates available online.

A professional looking résumé is one of the most important tools for your job hunt.

Any job involving food will look good on your résumé. Were you a barista? That involves inventory, recipes, and kitchen safety—all things chefs need.

You need to think of any experience that might be applicable. If you worked at a farmers' market selling produce or even on a farm, you can use this experience to demonstrate your familiarity with the farm-to-table ethic of modern cuisine. If you were a waiter or dishwasher in a restaurant previously, this can demonstrate your knowledge of how a kitchen works and your familiarity with restaurant hours. Even if you worked as a teller in a bank, the useful math skills you acquired can be relevant—chefs use a lot of math! These skills could also come in handy if you work in a smaller restaurant where you may be able to share responsibility for inventory management and balancing the books. Just remember, the most important thing about your résumé is that it conveys who you are, why you are passionate about food, and why you would be a good asset to any restaurant.

Make sure you do a lot of research on the restaurants you want to apply to. Study and memorize the menus, learn about the head chef, and read reviews. Visit the restaurant and order a meal if it's within your price range, or an appetizer or dessert if that's more affordable.

- Do you like the atmosphere?
- Is the staff inviting?
- Does the restaurant (including the parking lot) look clean?
- How about the restrooms?
- Does the food smell appetizing?

Remember, a job is more than a paycheck. You're looking for a place you really want to spend time in.

This is important both so you know if you want to apply there and can answer questions about why you want to work there if you get an interview. The people interviewing you will want to know why you chose their restaurant and what you are hoping to bring to the restaurant, as well as what you are hoping to take away from the experience. Successful chefs say that putting your résumé out there and waiting for interviews and job offers is an exercise in patience and persistence. It can take a long time and require a lot of legwork. The important thing is to not give up and to not take no for an answer.

If you can get an interview, be prepared to answer a lot of questions about your interest in food and what inspires you. As with any job interview, look neat and well groomed. Your hands should be

Unless it's a very fancy restaurant, or you're applying for a management position, you probably don't need to wear a suit for your interview. Business casual will probably work—just be neat and well groomed.

clean and your nails tidy—this is not an occasion for long acrylic claws! Be friendly and courteous to anyone you encounter on the property.

You might be asked where you've traveled and what flavors are your favorite. The interviewer will also likely be interested in your goals and where you would like to be in a few years. The point of the interview is both to see if you are a good fit for the restaurant and to see if the restaurant is a good fit for you. In the interview, as in the résumé, the best thing you can do is convey your passion for food and cooking. Don't worry as much about technical questions or knowing every possible cooking technique. Restaurants hiring new chefs are more concerned that you have the essential qualities and makings of a good chef, and that you'll fit in well with their staff. If you have the desire, will, passion, creativity, and basic talent required to be a chef, they will often be willing to train you on the job.

Your workstation should always be neat and orderly. This helps prevent mix-ups with orders. It also helps keep you and your coworkers safe from spills that can cause accidents.

Some restaurants ask applicants to "trail" in the restaurant before signing them on to work full-time. In some culinary programs, it's actually one of the requirements. Trailing basically means working for free at the restaurant so the chefs can see how well you mesh with the rest of the team and with the restaurant as a whole. Because line chefs must work together like a well-oiled machine to get everything done, it's very important that each new chef who is hired works well with the other chefs. Unpaid trailing might sound like a raw deal, but it's actually a great opportunity for the applicant. While the restaurant is determining if the chef is right for it, the chef can also use this time to determine if the restaurant is the right choice for them. Perhaps one restaurant is simply too busy to provide a good atmosphere for learning. Or maybe the kitchen looks like a great candidate for a restaurant makeover show. Trailing gives you a chance to see how the kitchen operates and if you'd prefer to work in a larger or smaller restaurant or one that serves a different style of food.

PUTTING YOUR BEST FOOT FORWARD

Whether you're trailing, apprenticing, or working your first job, it's important to make a good impression. You want to arrive on time, if not early, for your shift every day. If you're not on time, you will look disorganized, which is one thing no chef can afford to be. Employers expect you to be at your station, ready to work, at your start time, not just walking through the door with your coat on. Allow enough time to arrive and stow your belongings in your locker. Be reliable. Know what your schedule is and arrive prepared to work. (Don't stay out all night if you're scheduled for brunch service!) You should also be aware that in most work situations, the newest employees are often scheduled for weekends, holidays, and weird back-to-back shifts.

Restaurants have standards of presentation. You need to be consistent not only in how you prepare the food, but also how you plate it.

You'll learn a lot in school, but there's plenty more to learn after you land your first job.

It's important to make the best of on-the-job learning. Find a mentor who will help guide you and give you feedback. Feedback early in your career—both positive and negative—is important to any chef's growth and maturation as a culinary professional.

Equally important is learning to establish a daily plan that you can execute the same way every day. Take notes on each step you are responsible for and make sure you keep your quality consistent no matter what step in the process you're handling. A good chef will always keep thorough notes, with a prep list and a diagram of what their workstation will look like. You might think you can remember everything and not write things down, but keep in mind that the prep list and station diagram will be changing as the menu changes, so keeping notes is a good way to not get confused or miss something. Remember, customers have their favorite dishes and notice if something doesn't taste the same.

Your goal as a new chef is to be part of a great team, delivering great food. Whether you're making tacos in a food truck or decorating a cake for a high-society wedding, you want to do your very best.

REALITY TV

Televised cooking shows have come a long way from the days of Julia Child on PBS. Today, there are entire cable channels that broadcast nothing but cooking programs 24/7. They range from traditional formats, where a celebrity chef demonstrates their special recipes and techniques, to contests for established chefs or teams of newbies. There are programs that showcase some of the best restaurants in the country and others that make over the worst. Some even offer the chance to win a TV contract. These programs are very entertaining, and they can be a great way to keep up on the latest trends. Just remember that your chances of achieving overnight fame and fortune are slim. Building your skills through solid training and practice is much more likely to get you a satisfying career.

You can get some great ideas from cooking shows. You might learn about cuisines that aren't common where you live.

CHAPTER FIVE

WHAT'S ON THE HORIZON?

A good chef needs to be aware of all the latest trends in dining. Often these trends might be influenced by heads of state or celebrities. For example, the Obama White House was very focused on nutrition and fresh fruit and vegetables. This filtered down into what average Americans wanted to eat.

Even something as basic as a burger is subject to change. What if you crossed a burger with a quesadilla? Or used trendy bison meat instead of regular ground beef? Or no beef at all? The possibilities are endless, and a good chef needs to keep an open mind.

ORGANIC, LOCALLY SOURCED, AND FARM TO TABLE

Today, people are interested in eating healthy, nutritious foods, even when dining out. In recent years, peoples' ideas of healthy eating have extended to include eating in ways that are healthy for the Earth as well as themselves. They're willing to pay more for food that's better quality and obtained in ways that are better for the planet.

- Farmers grow organic food without synthetic pesticides, fertilizers, or genetically modified organisms (GMOs). This term can apply to produce, meat, and dairy products.
- Ethically sourced food is obtained via a supply chain where all employees at each step of the process are treated fairly and paid a reasonable wage (i.e.: no child labor or sweatshops). You'll often hear this in reference to coffee and chocolate.
- Vegan food contains no animal products. Ideally everything is plant based. Vegans generally do not eat dairy or even honey.

Locally sourced cuisine uses food products grown—you guessed it—locally. Some chefs even form partnerships with local farmers or routinely shop for their ingredients at farmers' markets. People enjoy knowing that by eating at a certain restaurant they will be supporting the local farmers in their community. They will also know that by eating there, the food is very fresh because it will not have had to travel very far and probably didn't need to be frozen.

It costs more money to fish responsibly, but killing animals protected by law can result in expensive fines. In addition, many people feel a connection to animals such as dolphins and bad publicity can be even more costly.

In addition to locally sourced and organic foods, there is an emerging culinary trend toward sustainable seafood. Seafood that is sustainable includes species of fish, shellfish, and mollusks that are not overharvested. There must be an abundance left in the ocean so the species isn't threatened by large-scale commercial fishing and harvesting. Additionally, fish that are farmed in ways that negatively impact the environment aren't considered sustainable.

Fisheries must be managed to reduce "bycatch." Bycatch are animals that aren't intended to be caught. This includes marine mammals and turtles that become tangled in nets and drowned. It also includes undersized fish or undesirable species. Removing too many of these from the water can disrupt the food chain in the area.

People also want to make sure other marine life, such as dolphins, aren't harmed in the process of catching fish. For seafood to be marketed as "dolphin safe," the captain of a fishing vessel must certify that they didn't use the sort of nets dolphins can become trapped in, and that no dolphins were harmed while bringing in their catch. Starting in 2016, captains must also complete a dolphin-safety training course.

There is also a rapidly growing interest in gluten-free menu items for gluten-sensitive and gluten-intolerant restaurant-goers. Adding a few gluten-free items to a menu can give a restaurant an edge over its competition as more and more people follow a gluten-free or gluten-reduced diet. However, chefs and servers need to be aware that while some people follow a gluten-free diet to be trendy, for others it's a very serious health concern.

TAPAS AND TECHNOLOGY

Another "big" trend in dining is "small plates." One of the best-known types of small plates are Spanish tapas. These are essentially appetizer-sized portions of things from olives, cheese, or sausage to portions of cooked fish or a slice of local quiche. Sometimes people order several tapas instead of a single entrée. In some places, instead of sitting down to a big meal, people go from one tapas bar to another, sampling lots of different dishes.

The idea of small plates crosses all types of cuisine, including Chinese. Dim sum is a similar concept to tapas. It consists of an assortment of dumplings and other small plates served with tea. It is becoming increasingly popular among diners as these scaled-down portions are being dished out more and more around the country.

Dim sum can be made of fish, meat, or vegetables. They're traditionally eaten for brunch.

FROM THE FARM TO THE TABLE

The farm-to-table movement is a growing trend in the restaurant industry. The idea is that everything served at a restaurant would be sourced locally and served fresh and in season. This would eliminate shipping, freezing, and preservatives from the process.

Some organizations take this a step further—or a step closer, if you will. They locate the restaurant at the farm. Stone Barns Center for Food and Agriculture is a working farm in Westchester County, New York. They raise sheep and cattle, and people driving along Bedford Road can often see the animals grazing. The center runs many tours and educational programs, and their sheep sometimes visit nearby historic Philipsburg Manor to participate in sheep-shearing demonstrations.

Blue Hill at Stone Barns is a unique fine-dining experience. The chef in residence creates meals from the fresh foods organically grown and produced on site. Blue Hill also operates a cafeteria that serves the same excellent ingredients in a more casual setting, and a market so guests can bring home special treats such as honey and jams created right there.

The advantage of dining in a farm-to-table establishment such as Blue Hill is knowing that your lamb chops were born on the same property where you're eating. The chefs know exactly what the lamb was fed for its entire life and when it was butchered.

Small plates are a fun concept for diners because they can enjoy a variety of tastes, instead of choosing just one entrée. It also has the added benefit of being very social, since small plates are often meant to be shared. While the model is customer friendly, it also works well for restaurants because, while each plate has smaller quantities of food and is often cheaper than an entrée, diners will often order several of them. Additionally, food can be served as soon as it is prepared. Serving a table of six people who have ordered traditionally sized entrées requires split-second timing and careful communication in the kitchen so that all six entrées are ready to go to the table at the same time. However, with small plates that will be shared by all the guests at the table, food can go out piping hot as soon as it's ready, requiring far less of a juggling act.

Small plates are fun because you can try lots of different things.

Molecular gastronomy is the scientific study of what happens to food on a molecular level during cooking. It's a discipline practiced by scientists in labs. However, some chefs have applied some molecular gastronomy discoveries to their cooking techniques. This is called molecular cooking or molecular cuisine.

Beyond the grill or oven, there are many advanced cooking techniques that chefs have only begun to explore. For example, chefs have been known to use molecular additives such as starch, pectin, or gelatin to create "novel foods." They can use liquid nitrogen for fast freezing. Another cooking method that has taken off in recent years is the sous vide method. Sous vide means "under vacuum." Using this method, food is cooked by sealing it in airtight plastic packages and submerging it in warm water for long periods of time. The intention is to cook the item evenly and avoid overcooking the outside, while keeping the inside at the same level of "doneness." This makes it easier to keep the food tender and juicy but still fully cooked.

WHAT DOES THE FUTURE HOLD?

According to the National Restaurant Association, the restaurant industry is on track to make $997 billion in 2023. The industry has a forecast of 500,000 new jobs, for total employment of 15.5 million. (This includes all types of food service employees—chefs, wait staff, dishwashers, managers, etc.) Those are some serious numbers!

About 63 percent of adults have worked in the restaurant industry at some point. That makes the industry a major player in the economy.

According to the BLS, there are over 174,000 chefs and head cooks employed in the United States. More than half of them work in restaurants. They can expect to earn about $56,000 per year. There are expected to be 9,000 new positions in the next decade, allowing for faster growth than most other career paths. The BLS reports an additional 2.7 million cooks. About three-quarters of them work in restaurants and other eateries. They earn about $31,000 per year and can also expect faster than average growth of about 175,000 new jobs over the next decade.

About 15 percent of chefs and head cooks work in hotels, amusement, or gambling venues. Some even work on cruise ships!

Years ago, many women were stay-at-home moms. They didn't work outside the home, so they had plenty of time to plan meals, shop, cook, and clean up. Eating out at a restaurant was a treat for special occasions. Today, all the adults in most households work. While dining out at a nice restaurant is still a favorite way to celebrate, grabbing food that someone else cooked at the end of a long workday is much more common. Even if it's takeout or a pizza, working people are happy to pay for something they don't have to prepare themselves.

While not all chef and food preparation jobs are recession-proof, there is a great deal of growth in the restaurant industry. The U.S. Department of Agriculture (USDA) attributed 10.5 percent of U.S. employment to food and food-related industries. This included 11.8 million jobs in food services.

From fast food to fine dining, Americans love their restaurants. Do you have what it takes to be the person preparing that great dining experience?

Becoming a chef is a great way to share your passion for food with others.

If you're passionate about food and not afraid of hard work, a career as a chef might be the right choice for you. You can work anywhere from a school to a diner to a luxury cruise ship. Maybe you want to help people celebrate their biggest milestones. Or maybe you want to dish up good, old-fashioned comfort food to folks at the end of a long day. The possibilities are endless, and once you have training and a solid skill set, you'll have the tools to explore more than one path.

Most people choose to become a chef because they simply love to cook, but if you eventually decide to leave the kitchen, there are still many options. You might decide to write about food or create your own cookbook. You could go back to school to become qualified as a nutritionist. You could even teach the next generation of chefs. Who knows? Maybe you'll even be the next chef with your very own TV show and merchandise.

10 GREAT QUESTIONS TO ASK A CHEF

Here are some questions you can ask a chef. Try to speak to chefs who work in different venues to get different perspectives.

1. Did you attend culinary school or some other type of training?
2. Why did you choose it?
3. There are a lot of cooking and food magazines. Which ones do you recommend?
4. Do you have a favorite celebrity chef?
5. Are there any cookbooks that are must-reads?
6. Is this the only setting you've worked in?
7. What's your dream job?
8. Are there any classes or extracurricular activities I should be taking now?
9. Do you belong to any professional organizations?
10. What's your favorite thing to cook?

What other questions can you think of?

With time, training, and practice you can master even the most difficult cooking styles!

GLOSSARY

ambience: The mood or atmosphere created by an environment.

apprenticeship: The system in which a person learns a craft through mentoring by a master of that craft.

chain restaurant: A restaurant that has many different locations and is owned or overseen by a parent company.

chef de partie: A chef who is in charge of a particular station in a kitchen. Sometimes known as a station cook or line cook.

commis: An assistant to a chef; usually considered a training position.

culinary: Of or relating to cooking.

executive chef: The chef who has the top authority in the kitchen, sometimes known as the head chef.

expediting: Helping to pace cooking so that dishes all leave the kitchen at the right time.

externship: Working in a restaurant, either paid or unpaid, as a learning experience. Similar to an internship but often shorter in duration.

franchise: A business that the owner is allowed to run under the auspices and oversight of a larger corporation.

garde-manger: A chef who manages cold items, such as salads or cold appetizers.

knife skills: Part of a chef's skill set, dealing with different techniques for cutting and chopping.

line cook: A chef who is in charge of a particular station in a kitchen. Sometimes known as a station cook or chef de partie.

local: Food that is grown or produced close to where it is consumed.

organic: Food that is grown in an environment free of pesticides and chemicals.

prep cook: A chef who helps ready ingredients for other chefs to cook.

sous-chef: The second-in-command in a kitchen under the head chef.

station cook: A chef who is assigned to work at a specific station within a kitchen. Sometimes known as a line cook or chef de partie.

sustainable: Food that is grown, raised, or harvested with minimal impact on the environment.

toque: A tall, white hat traditionally worn by chefs.

trailing: Working in a restaurant on a trial basis, usually without being paid.

FOR MORE INFORMATION

AMERICAN CULINARY FEDERATION (ACF)

6816 Southpoint Pkwy.
Ste. 400
Jacksonville, FL 32216
(904) 824-4468
Website: www.acfchefs.org
Facebook: @ACFChefs
Instagram: @ACF_CHEFS
The ACF is the largest professional chefs' organization in North America.

AUGUSTE ESCOFFIER SCHOOL OF CULINARY ARTS

637 South Broadway
Suite H
Boulder, CO 80305
(877) 249-0305
Website: www.escoffier.edu
Facebook and YouTube: @escoffierschool
Instagram: @escoffierschools
Named for renowned chef Auguste Escoffier, the Escoffier School has two world-class campuses and an online culinary program.

CULINARY INSTITUTE OF AMERICA (CIA)

1946 Campus Drive
Hyde Park, NY 12538-1499
(845) 452-9600
Website: www.ciachef.edu
Facebook: @CIAchef
Instagram: @theculinaryinstituteofamerica
YouTube: @culinaryinstituteofamerica
The CIA is the oldest culinary school in the United States and one of the most prestigious in the world.

CULINARY INSTITUTE OF CANADA AT HOLLAND COLLEGE (CIC)

140 Weymouth Street
Charlottetown, Prince Edward Island
Canada C1A 4Z1
(902) 894-6868
Website: www.hollandcollege.com/about/campuses-and-centres/the-culinary-institute-of-canada
Facebook and Instagram: @HollandCollege
The CIC offers programs in the culinary arts, as well as hotel and restaurant management and event planning. Students operate a cafeteria and restaurant.

NEW ENGLAND CULINARY ARTS TRAINING (NECAT)

23 Bradston Street
Boston, MA 02118
(617) 442-3600
Website: www.ne-cat.org/
Facebook: @BostonNECAT
NECAT is a non-profit organization that offers culinary training and career assistance to adults.

INSTITUTE OF CULINARY EDUCATION (ICE)

225 Liberty Street
3rd Floor
New York, NY 10281
(888) 354-CHEF
Website: www.iceculinary.com
Facebook, Instagram, and YouTube: @iceculinary
The ICE is an award-winning culinary school with campuses in New York City and Los Angeles.

JAMES BEARD FOUNDATION

167 West 12th Street
New York, NY 10011
(212) 627-2308
Website: www.jamesbeard.org
Facebook and Instagram: @beardfoundation
The James Beard Foundation is a nonprofit organization that sponsors culinary scholarships, as well as prestigious annual awards.

JOB CORPS

200 Constitution Avenue NW, Room N4459
Washington, D.C. 20210
(800) 733-JOBS [5627]
Website: www.jobcorps.gov
Facebook and Instagram: @DOLJobCorps
The Job Corps is a Department of Labor program that provides free job training for young people. They offer several options in the food industry.

NO KID HUNGRY

1030 15th St, NW
Washington DC 20005
(888) 969-4767
Website: www.nokidhungry.org/
Facebook and Instagram: @nokidhungry
No Kid Hungry is the arm of Share Our Strength committed to combating childhood hunger through school and community meals.

SHARE OUR STRENGTH

1030 15th St, NW
Washington DC 20005
(888) 903-8261
Website: www.shareourstrength.org/
Share Our Strength is an organization dedicated to ending childhood hunger through food and nutrition education.

FOR FURTHER READING

Gluckstern, Rachel. *Working in Restaurants and Catering*. Buffalo, NY: Rosen Young Adult, 2019.

Hamilton, Tracy. *Culinary Arts: A Practical Career Guide*. Lanham, MD: Rowman & Littlefield, 2019.

Mahoney, Ellen. *Food Stars: 15 Women Stirring Up the Food Industry*. Chicago, IL: Chicago Review Press, 2023.

Mangani, Marisa. *Mise en Place: Memoir of a Girl Chef*. Austin, TX: River Grove Books, 2022.

Marlowe, Christie, and Andrew Morkes. *Chef: A Culinary Artist*. Hollywood, FL: Mason Crest, 2020.

Mooney, Carla. *The Chemistry of Food*. Ashland, VT: Nomad Press, 2021.

Natera, Andre. *Chef's PSA: How Not to Be the Biggest Idiot in the Kitchen*. Independently Published, 2022.

Williams, Morgan. *Careers for People Who Love Cooking*. Buffalo, NY: Rosen Publishing, 2021.

INDEX

E

F

G

H

I

J

S

T

U

W

ABOUT THE AUTHOR

KATHLEEN A. KLATTE is the author of many nonfiction books for children and teens. Topics range from animals and nature to constitutional law to unusual career choices. She lives in New York with one cat and far too many books and Legos.

PHOTO CREDITS

Photo credits: Cover, pp. 1, 34 Drazen Zigic/Shutterstock.com; pp. 3-96 Merydolla/Shutterstock.com; p. 4 Tyler Olson/Shutterstock.com; p. 6 Skylines/Shutterstock.com; p. 7 Radiokafka/Shutterstock.com; p. 9 AlessandroBiascioli/Shutterstock.com; p. 11 melissamn/Shutterstock.com; p. 13 Gorodenkoff/Shutterstock.com; p. 14 ZoranOrcik/Shutterstock.com; p. 15 SaiArLawKa2/Shutterstock.com; p. 17 kittirat roekburi/Shutterstock.com; p. 18 Pavel L Photo and Video/Shutterstock.com; p. 19 Jacob Lund/Shutterstock.com; p. 20 Suprun Vitaly/Shutterstock.com; p. 21 wavebreakmedia/Shutterstock.com; p. 22 ESB Professional/Shutterstock.com; p. 23 hxdbzxy/Shutterstock.com; p. 25 vectorfusionart/Shutterstock.com; p. 27 Gagarin Iurii/Shutterstock.com; p. 29 monticello/Shutterstock.com; p. 30 ercan senkaya/Shutterstock.com; p. 32 H_Sutthichai/Shutterstock.com; p. 35 Anna Shepulova/Shutterstock.com; p. 36 Leonardo Moreno C/Shutterstock.com; p. 37 Monkey Business Images/Shutterstock.com; p. 38 David Tadevosian/Shutterstock.com; p. 39 Yevgeniy Melnik/Shutterstock.com; p. 41 New Africa/Shutterstock.com; p. 43 Depiction Images/Shutterstock.com; p. 44 Nancy Kennedy/Shutterstock.com; p. 46 Parilov/Shutterstock.coml; p. 48 360b/Shutterstock.com; p. 49 https://commons.wikimedia.org/wiki/File:Andre_Rush_2019_(48647848408).jpg; p. 5 1 Ekkasit A Siam/Shutterstock.com; p. 53 Timolina/Shutterstock.com; p. 55 Estrada Anton/Shutterstock.com; p. 57 Minerva Studio/Shutterstock.com; p. 58 Pixel-Shot/Shutterstock.com; p. 59 Jacob Lund/Shutterstock.com ; p. 60 Nikolai Hamel / Alamy Stock Photo; p. 62 JeniFoto/Shutterstock.com; p. 63 Andrey_Popov/Shutterstock.com; p. 64 Rawpixel.com/Shutterstock.com; p. 65 Pranithan Chorruangsak/Shutterstock.com; p. 66 djile/Shutterstock.com; p. 67 Rawpixel.com/Shutterstock.com; p. 69 wavebreakmedia/Shutterstock.com; p. 70 anon_tae/Shutterstock.com; p. 71 II.studio/Shutterstock.com; p. 73 New Africa/Shutterstock.com; p. 75 josua royto panggabean/Shutterstock.com; p. 76 Lakeview Images/Shutterstock.com; p. 77 Gulcin Ragiboglu/Shutterstock.com; p. 79 Salvador Aznar/Shutterstock.com; p. 80 DGLimages/Shutterstock.com; p. 81 LightField Studios/Shutterstock.com; p. 83 Aleksandr_Alekseev/Shutterstock.com.